Church Wounds
Copyright © 2023 by Lindsay Denham

All rights reserved. No part of this publication may be reproduced, distributed, or transmitted in any form or by any means, including photocopying, recording, or other electronic or mechanical methods, without the prior written permission of the author, except in the case of brief quotations embodied in critical reviews and certain other non-commercial uses permitted by copyright law.

All Scripture quotations, unless otherwise indicated, are taken from the Holy Bible, New International Version®, NIV®. Copyright ©1973, 1978, 1984, 2011 by Biblica, Inc.™ Used by permission of Zondervan. All rights reserved worldwide. www.zondervan.com The "NIV" and "New International Version" are trademarks registered in the United States Patent and Trademark Office by Biblica, Inc.™

Scripture quotations marked (AMP) are taken from the Amplified Bible, Copyright © 2015 by The Lockman Foundation. Used by permission.

Scripture taken from *THE MESSAGE*. Copyright © 1993, 1994, 1995, 1996, 2000, 2001, 2002. Used by permission of NavPress Publishing Group.

Scripture taken from The Voice™. Copyright © 2012 by Ecclesia Bible Society. Used by permission. All rights reserved.

Scripture quotations marked (NLT) are taken from the *Holy Bible*, New Living Translation, copyright ©1996, 2004, 2015 by Tyndale House Foundation. Used by permission of Tyndale House Publishers, Carol Stream, Illinois 60188. All rights reserved.

Scripture quotations taken from the (NASB®) New American Standard Bible®, Copyright © 1960, 1971, 1977, 1995, by The Lockman Foundation. Used by permission. All rights reserved. www.lockman.org

Tellwell Talent
www.tellwell.ca

ISBN
978-0-2288-8776-8 (Paperback)
978-0-2288-8777-5 (eBook)

# TABLE OF CONTENTS

Preface.................................................................................................. v

Who this Book is For........................................................................ xv

Applicable Verses......................................................................... xvii

Format............................................................................................. xxi

Chapter 1: The Formative Years...................................................... 1
    Exercise 1: The Formative Years .................................................. 3

Chapter 2: Church Experiences..................................................... 10
    Exercise 2: Personal Church Experience .................................. 12

Chapter 3: Witnessing the Church Experiences of Others.......... 29
    Exercise 3: Witnessing the Church Experiences of Others......... 31

Chapter 4: Serving in Leadership.................................................. 48
    Exercise 4: Serving in Leadership ............................................. 50

Chapter 5: Family Relationships with Church Leaders
       (Paid or Volunteer) .............................................................. 60
    Exercise 5: Family Relationships with Church Leaders
       (Paid or Volunteer) ....................................................... 62

Chapter 6: Blaming God.................................................................. 70
    Exercise 6: Blaming God ............................................................ 72

In Conclusion.................................................................................. 74

# PREFACE

I am a huge proponent of ministries that help people walk in the freedom that Jesus died for them to receive, enjoy, and flourish under. A couple years ago I received an intercessory word from the Lord during prayer regarding His Father's heart and desire for synergy among His children, and there being no room for dissention, gossip, slander, and dishonour in His Church. This past year I was continually bombarded by Scriptures that referred to the body of Christ, unity, loving your brothers and sisters in Christ, forgiving one another, and bearing with one another in love. At that point it wasn't surprising to me when I felt the Holy Spirit reveal the vital connection between His desire for His Church and the need for a healing ministry that deals specifically with woundedness that has occurred because of other Christians or church in general. After all, the Church is His beloved bride that He cherishes and sacrificed for, and He wants her to be beautiful and holy. He is more than worthy of such a bride, so if that is what He esteems and desires, that is what our hearts should long for and aim for as well. But we have a huge part to play in that.

Jesus summarizes His calling for us by reducing all the commands to just two, first, "Love the Lord your God" and second, "Love your neighbor" (Matthew 22:37-39). So simple! Yet our woundedness and sin interfere with this perfect love. Wounded people tend to wound people, and therefore within churches, just as within families, there can be sensitivities, unfair expectations, differences in opinions, jealousy, exclusion, judgment, rejection, criticism, accusation, favoritism, contention, division, and splits, which can leave people feeling less than loved, accepted, or safe. Most of us would agree that in a church setting there can be a level of expectancy that there will be love, grace, safety, acceptance, and a sort of *Kumbaya* environment. That's not wrong, and with childlike faith I believe it should and can be that way, but that expectation can also throw people for a loop when any sign of disharmony rears its ugly head. I have heard people caution, "There are no perfect churches," and since churches are hospitals for the soul comprised of the spiritually sick in need of wellness, perhaps we shouldn't be surprised that people might get spiritually vomited on from time to time. If you have been part of a church, you have likely experienced that to some degree.

Some people's defense could arguably be, "That's why I don't go to church! I can love God and live for Him away from the organized church." There's some truth to that, but is that really God's intention for any of us or for His Church? I'm quite certain our beloved brothers and sisters in Christ locked away in isolated prison cells for their faith wouldn't think so. Consider these challenging words from Paul, "Whoever claims to love God yet hates a brother or sister is a liar" (1 John 4:20). Many tend to regard "hate" as a strong word so readily defend that they don't *hate* any Christian brothers and sisters, but the original meaning of the word suggests that hostility toward, aversion to, and animosity towards, are also parts of its definition. We are instructed in Hebrews 10:25, "Let's see how inventive we can be in encouraging love and helping out, not avoiding worshiping together as some do but spurring each other on, especially as we see the big Day approaching" (THE MESSAGE).

Verse after verse in Scripture promote the fact that as Christ followers, we are no longer orphans, alone, but instead are part of a new family that we play a specific roll within. "For just as each of us has one body with many members, and these members do not all have the same function, so in Christ we, though many, form one body, and each member belongs to all the others" (Romans 12:4-5). Each one is called to participate to, "strive to excel in ways that will build up the church spiritually" (1 Cor 14:12, AMP), "so that there should be no division in the body, but that its parts should have equal concern for each other" (1 Corinthians 12:25). We are part of this body, and the gifts God gives us are to be used for the greater glory, within, and then outside the church.

Brothers and sisters; family. Consider how important family is in an earthly sense. Its importance crosses cultures, time, education, social circles, and economic factors. Since God has placed within us this innate value for earthly family, it makes sense that He would use these earthly relationships to demonstrate something deeper with respect to spiritual relationships in His Kingdom. In these earthly relationships we have our first opportunities to learn about love, grace, perseverance, personalities, cooperation, compromise, and conflict resolution. In our Kingdom relationships, especially during tough times, we have opportunities for spiritual growth so that we can become mature sons and daughters. We need the church for this and are instructed how to go about it in 2 Peter 1:5-9 (The Voice):

> 'To achieve this, you will need to add virtue to your faith, and then knowledge to your virtue; to knowledge, add discipline; to discipline, add endurance; to endurance, add godliness; to godliness, add affection for others as sisters and brothers; and to affection, at last, add love. For if you possess these traits and multiply them, then you will never be ineffective or unproductive in your relationship with our Lord Jesus the Anointed; but if you don't have these qualities, then you will be nearsighted and blind, forgetting that your past sins have been washed away."

We are warned, "Now for a little while you may have had to suffer grief in all kinds of trials. These have come so that the proven genuineness of your faith—of greater worth than gold, which perishes even though refined by fire—may result in praise, glory, and honor when Jesus Christ is revealed." (1 Peter 1:6, 7).

Scripture tells us we are God's children (1 John 3:1), a chosen race (1 Peter 2:9), members of God's household (Ephesians 2:19), joint heirs (Romans 8:17), and we are called to be *one* (John 17:21-22). When the Church functions as God intended, take into account what happens:

> "They devoted themselves to the apostles' teaching and to fellowship, to the breaking of bread and to prayer.

Everyone was filled with awe at the many wonders and signs performed by the apostles. All the believers were together and had everything in common. They sold property and possessions to give to anyone who had need. Every day they continued to meet together in the temple courts. They broke bread in their homes and ate together with glad and sincere hearts, praising God and enjoying the favor of all the people. And the Lord added to their number daily those who were being saved." (Acts 2:42-47).

Even with this beautiful picture of the Church at her finest, it wasn't long before selfishness, dishonesty, favoritism, and discontentment emerged in Acts 5 and 6. God wants more for His bride, and that comes through refining, growth, forgiveness, perseverence, cooperation, and maturity.

Therefore, it is with wisdom that Paul, in Ephesians 4:3, avers, "Make every effort to keep the unity of the Spirit through the bond of peace." I used to think this effort meant trying harder to overlook, repress, and just get over any mistreatment I felt I had experienced. Now, I am more and more convinced it means making the effort to invite Holy Spirit to search my heart so I can deal with things that have happened and any potential woundedness associated with it by acknowledging the misdemeanor (real or perceived), identifying feelings that surface, repenting of any associated lies that may have taken root, replacing lies with the truth that comes from God, forgiving those that may have played a role, and perhaps going to others to make peace.

I included the bracketed phrase "real or perceived" in the previous paragraph because this can play an important role in the healing process. Please be assured I am not suggesting your situation wasn't real, that it didn't cause pain, or that there wasn't some sort of mistreatment involved. What I am saying is that we must consider if any perceptions we have had, with regard to a situation or comment, could have caused us to misinterpret anything. Miscommunication is a real thing and can show up in different ways. Let me share three examples.

First, I recall a situation where a young lady, Shanaya, was attending college full-time, working a part-time job, and volunteering with the weekly children's program at her church when her pastor asked her if she would volunteer with the new monthly girl's program. Based on what I know about the situation, I believe the conversations went something like this:

> Pastor: *Shanaya, the church leadership has decided it's time to start a girl's night. It will only be once a month, and we think you would be the best volunteer for it.*

> Shanaya: *Aww, thanks. I think starting a girl's night is an awesome idea. Let me think about it and pray about it and I will get back to you.*

A few days later, Shanaya returned to the church to meet with the pastor.

> Shanaya: *A few days after we talked, I ended up having a small panic attack. It made me realize my schedule is too full and I need to figure out how to manage my time better. I love working with the kids and I'm so blessed by them, but I don't think I can take on girl's night right now.*

> Pastor: *Oh Shanaya, I'm so sorry to hear the stress of things is getting to you. I knew your schedule was busy, and I do hope you will find a way to manage your time better for the sake of your mental health, but I still hope you'll consider being involved in the girl's night. I mean it's only one night per month.*

> Shanaya: *Well, I don't think I can manage that, so I guess I have to step down from volunteering for a while.*

> Pastor: *But you love working with the kids and the girls love you so much, and it's only one night per month.*

> Shanaya: *I'm sorry, I can't do that. In fact, I think I will be taking a break from the church for a while.*

Miscommunication abounded leaving both parties questioning how well they knew the other, and both felt wounded by the situation. The pastor had been encouraged by the board to expand the weekly children's program so that the girls and boys could meet separately once per month. Because of Shanaya's busy schedule and reputation with the kids, he thought she should be the first person asked to help with the monthly girl's night. That way, she could lessen her volunteer hours from weekly to monthly but still be involved with the young girls she was blessed by. When asked to help with the girl's program, Shanaya figured the pastor was asking her to do it *in addition* to the children's program and thought it would be a lot with her schedule, but loved the idea of being able to be with the girls the extra day. After the panic attack, however, she knew she couldn't take on more hours of volunteering so mentally wrote off the idea of participating in the girl's night. When, after informing the pastor about the panic attack and the pastor being so insistent about her involvement in girl's night, she felt pressured, so quickly responded that she would be stepping down from volunteering. As the pastor persisted, Shanaya was baffled by his insensitivity to her situation and out of frustration and concern about this character flaw decided she would have to take a break from the church. The pastor was left dumbfounded, convinced she would be thrilled for the one night per month volunteer opportunity. She ended up leaving not only the young girls she loved to minister to but taking a break from the church. Serious miscommunication.

The second example of miscommunication comes in the form of misinformation and a lack of information. A young lady, Lori, with a variety of abilities and a willingness to serve wherever there was a need was serving as the volunteer children's program co-ordinator when suddenly the church hired a full-time staff member to do the job. Lori heard from several reliable people that this new person was hired because the board wanted the children's program to grow and expand. Lori was slightly disappointed that the board didn't even offer her the challenge of expanding the program and felt uneasy about the stewardship of church finances and paying this new hire to do what she was willing to do for free. What Lori didn't know was that the head pastor's wife was experiencing health challenges and as a result he was needing somebody to help relieve the demands of the preaching schedule as well as help with some of his pastoral duties. What Lori also didn't know was that there was concern about the middle school program co-ordinator who was going to be asked to step down for a time because of an affair he was involved in that had just recently been discovered by his wife. After that was dealt with, the board was planning to ask Lori if she would make the transition from the children's program to the middle school program. Because of the confidential nature of the circumstances, Lori couldn't be given all the information and was temporarily left in the dark, but fortunately she was patient and gracious about the situation, though internally she had to work through some of her frustration and confusion.

The third example comes from a time when I was attending a ladies bible study and a couple weeks into the study one of my friends came. I greeted her and said how good it was to see her there. Within a couple weeks, I noticed she became distant and cold towards me. I asked her if there was anything I had done to offend her, but she said there wasn't, until about two years later when she finally admitted to me that she had interpreted me saying, "It's so good to see you" (aka I'm glad you're here), as, "It's so good to see you" (aka It's so good you finally dragged your sorry butt out of bed to come). I was so thankful that she eventually realized I had meant well, but it was her perception that led her to misinterpret what I had said, and it was easy for her to do because she was already feeling personal guilt and shame for not attending more regularly.

This guilt and shame provided the perfect breeding ground for misinterpretation that would lead to sensitivity, offense, resentment, and division. This breeding ground is the kind of thing we want to be aware of so that it can be identified and dealt with, perhaps in a personal inner healing session (or Sozo[1]), which I would recommend if

---

[1]    Sozo, derived from Greek, means whole, healed, saved and delivered, and is the name of one specific personal inner healing and deliverance ministry I would recommend. The book *Sozo: Saved, Healed, Delivered* is written by Teresa Liebscher and Dawna DeSilva; Published by Destiny Image; 2016. A Sozo session can be booked through some local churches or on the website @ www.bethelsozo.com

certain responses (anger, guilt, shame, rejection, disappointment etc.), or thought patterns ("I'm not good enough," "Nobody cares about me," "I always get left out," "They think I'm dumb," "They don't understand me", etc.), seem to repeatedly crop up in daily life and/or within the body of Christ.

It's important for us to realize that sometimes (I'm not saying it's always the case) the issues we have within the church are simply exposing a pre-existing sensitivity we have. If I grew up in a home where guilt and shame were the prime motivators to get me to perform or behave appropriately, that tendency can transfer to other situations, such as in the church, and make me feel like I'm being guilted or shamed to be a better Christian or serve more. I would need to do some prayerful personal reflection and healing to get free from those patterns. Those wounds weren't incurred by the church. The church simply brought them to light, which isn't a bad thing, because, "Everything exposed by the light becomes visible" (Ephesians 5:13).

In Ephesians 4 Paul says, "Don't give the devil a foothold," but not dealing with insecurity, guilt and shame, unworthiness, rejection, bitterness, lies that have been hurled at us, hurts that have accumulated, and resentment that ensues, does just that by providing a breeding ground that caters to Satan's work. The breeding ground has been further primed by society. Woke culture has been arousing heightened sensitivities and entitling those who have been wronged in any way to be offended. Cancel culture has encouraged followers to stand for justice and boycott leaders and organizations. Both ideologies have permeated the church and the consequences become evident as exasperation rises and attendance decreases. I don't think we give enough consideration to the fact there is an enemy behind it all who will go to every effort to thwart the plans of God. "For our struggle is not against flesh and blood, but against the rulers, against the authorities, against the powers of this dark world and against the spiritual forces of evil in the heavenly realms" (Ephesians 6:12). What better way of doing that than by attacking His children and His bride? Satan's desire is to harm the Church by breaking her down, individual by individual, and ruin her purity, integrity, unity, and reputation. When individuals aren't walking in the freedom Jesus died for them to have, ultimately the Church can't either.

I want to reassure you that this process is not about blame. There is no intention of pointing fingers at different people and using them as a scapegoat for any of your spiritual issues or shortcomings (and if you do get excited about pointing fingers at these people, that is a certain indicator it is a good time to go through a personal inner healing session…just saying). It is, however, recognizing that these people, well-intentioned or not, may have left a negative impact on you that is giving the devil a foothold and causing you to build walls and hindering your faith walk, your trust in God, your attitude towards your brothers and sisters, and overall unity and function in the body of Christ. This needs to get reconciled. That way, if something similar happens again, any future offense can land on fresh soil; not the kind that is already contaminated and therefore immediately allows for weeds of defensiveness, frustration, resentment, disappointment, self-preservation, hostility, and disunity.

Jesus came, "that we might have life, and have it to the full" (John 10:10), yet most believers aren't living, "filled to the measure of all the fullness of God" (Ephesians 3:19). Inner healing is about having people saved, healed, delivered, and made whole, and when we are, it can't help but make a difference in us as individuals and therefore the Church as a whole. We are called to be full to the measure of Christ and to be the salt and light of the world. We want to see the lost found and the captives set free. We want to see the harvest brought in. We want the sick healed, the dead raised, the lepers cleansed, and the demons driven out. We want to see His Kingdom come on earth as it is in Heaven. We want revival!!!

As your sister in Christ, I want to encourage you to be fully healed and free, in every area of your life, so you can experience more of the fullness of Christ and in turn successfully participate in bringing the Kingdom on earth as it is in Heaven. That involves, "finding out if there's any offensive way" (Psalm 139:23), in yourself so you can, "walk in the way everlasting" (Psalm 139:24). I want to thank you for considering going

xiii

through this process, and I pray you will, because it's not easy. "He will sit like a refiner of silver, burning away the dross" (Malachi 3:3, NLT). Becoming aware of footholds helps free us to be the joyful, loving, high functioning, full, encouraging, contributing part of the body of Christ He has called us to be, since, "From Him the whole body, joined and held together by every supporting ligament, grows and builds itself up as each part does its work" (Ephesians 4:16). Not only that, but we want the Church to be the testimony of God's goodness and power here on earth as we go and make disciples of all nations and so that the body of Christ can be presented to Him as the pure, holy, and radiant bride (Ephesians 5:27).

Lord, let Your Kingdom come on earth as it is in Heaven!!!

*But he was pierced for our transgressions, he was crushed for our iniquities; the punishment that brought us peace was on him, and by his wounds we are healed.*

*Isaiah 53:5*

# WHO THIS BOOK IS FOR

I recommend this workbook for *anybody* who considers themselves a follower of Jesus; i.e. a new Christian, a long time Christian (attending formal church or not attending a church), wants to join a ministry team, be part of a leadership team, become a church member, or join on staff. I especially recommend it if you know you have been hurt within the church, if you are jaded in any way towards church or Christians, or if you get defensive if somebody suggests you might need inner healing. You probably do. We all do.

I recommend this workbook as a tool for pastors and leaders to not just go through themselves, but to encourage their coworkers, deacons and elders, members, and volunteers to go through *before* they are given a platform of leadership within that church body. I recognize that a book of this sort could initially cause a pastor or ministry leader to feel like they might be put in a vulnerable position where people might end up pointing fingers at them since they are often the ones who make decisions that impact the people in their church, and this book does address how people have been impacted. I can identify with the passing thought, "Why would I recommend a book that might bring to light things I may have done that could suggest that I have failed the people I'm trying my best to love and serve?" My desire is not to make pastors or leaders feel more scrutinized or get attacked more than they already are. My desire is that congregants and leaders will each welcome Holy Spirit to come and reveal their part in any tension (where they have been hurt, how it made them feel, what lies they have believed, where miscommunication could have played a part, where any personal insecurities may have accentuated a situation, where they may be allowing bitterness to take root), and forgive those they feel may have contributed towards any hurts they have experienced and get healed by acknowledging and experiencing the truth that sets them free. Doing this, they will advance in spiritual strength and have <u>more</u> respect and honour for their leaders, those trying to do their best to shepherd their flocks, and for their brothers and sisters in Christ, in order to bring growth, wholeness, and unity, rather than frustration and division. There might be situations where somebody does come to you to try to seek reconciliation and my prayer is that both parties will extend love, grace, and wisdom, to bring about peace in the relationship and restoration to the body. "Blessed are the peacemakers" (Matthew 5:9).

It is *not* my desire to see brothers and sisters having to jump through hoops to serve in a church body, but it *is* my desire to see each person, specifically those involved in ministry, serve with maturity and a pure heart that isn't burdened by past wounds so they can contribute to the unity of the Spirit flowing by loving their brothers and sisters well, respecting and honouring their leaders as Christ calls us to do (1 Thessalonians 5:12-13; Hebrews 13:17), and handling with openness, wisdom, maturity, and grace any comments, suggestions, criticisms, differing opinions, contentions, or if necessary, correction. This is all in the name of protecting pastors and congregations and the whole bride of Christ from being re-assaulted by lingering hurts, bitterness, or offense obtained elsewhere, or in the past. If it doesn't get dealt with, it has the potential to give the enemy a foothold and bring all sorts of discontentment, contention, slander, and division.

I believe it will be very beneficial for brothers and sisters in Christ to go through these exercises each year to make sure nothing new has popped up that is leaving a bitter root. Ideally, we all want to get to a point where we can quickly recognize when a situation could lead to any kind of wounding or offense and deal with it immediately with awareness, forgiveness, wisdom, and God's truth. "Settle matters quickly" (Matthew 5:25).

# APPLICABLE VERSES

*Jesus said, "My prayer is not for them alone. I pray also for those who will believe in me through their message, that all of them may be one, Father, just as you are in me and I am in you. May they also be in us so that the world may believe that you have sent me. I have given them the glory that you gave me, that they may be one as we are one— I in them and you in me—so that they may be brought to complete unity. Then the world will know that you sent me and have loved them even as you have loved me.*

*John 17:20-23*

*A brother offended is harder to be won than a strong city, and contentions are like the bars of a citadel.*

*Proverbs 18:19 (NASB 1995)*

*A person's wisdom yields patience; it is to one's glory to overlook an offense.*

*Proverbs 19:11*

*At that time many will turn away from the faith and will betray and hate each other, and many false prophets will appear and deceive many people. Because of the increase of wickedness, the love of most will grow cold, but the one who stands firm to the end will be saved.*

*Matthew 24:10-13*

*See to it that no one falls short of the grace of God and that no bitter root grows up to cause trouble and defile many.*

*Hebrews 12:15*

*I can do all this through him who gives me strength.*

*Philippians 4:13*

*Search me, God, and know my heart; test me and know my anxious thoughts. See if there is any offensive way in me and lead me in the way everlasting.*

*Psalm 139:23-24*

*Do not judge, or you too will be judged. For in the same way you judge others, you will be judged, and with the measure you use, it will be measured to you. Why do you look at the speck of sawdust in your brother's eye and pay no attention to the plank in your own eye? First take the plank out of your own eye.*

*Matthew 7:1-3, 5*

*Do not merely listen to the Word and so deceive yourselves. Do what it says.*

*James 1:22*

*Finally, brothers and sisters, rejoice! Strive for full restoration, encourage one another, be of one mind, live in peace. And the God of love and peace will be with you.*

*2 Corinthians 13:11*

*If it is possible, as far as it depends on you, live at peace with everyone.*

*Romans 12:18*

*Let us therefore make every effort to do what leads to peace and to mutual edification.*

*Romans 14:19*

*Blessed are the peacemakers, for they will be called children of God.*

*Matthew 5:9*

*As a prisoner for the Lord, then, I urge you to live a life worthy of the calling you have received. Be completely humble and gentle; be patient, bearing with one another in love. Make every effort to keep the unity of the Spirit through the bond of peace. There is one body and one Spirit, just as you were called to one hope when you were called; one Lord, one faith, one baptism; one God and Father of all, who is over all and through all and in all.*

*Ephesians 4:1-6*

*Bear with each other and forgive one another if any of you has a grievance against someone. Forgive as the Lord forgave you. And over all these virtues put on love, which binds them all together in perfect unity.*

*Colossians 3:13-14*

*Make my joy complete by being like-minded, having the same love, being one in spirit and of one mind.*

*Philippians 2:2*

*I appeal to you, brothers and sisters, in the name of our Lord Jesus Christ, that all of you agree with one another in what you say and that there be no divisions among you, but that you be perfectly united in mind and thought.*

*1 Corinthians 1:10*

*Live in true devotion to one another, loving each other as sisters and brothers. Be first to honor others by putting them first. Take every opportunity to open your life and home to others. Work toward unity, and live in harmony with one another.*

*Romans 12:10, 13 & 16 (The Voice)*

*All the believers were one in heart and mind.*

*Acts 4:32*

*So Christ himself gave the apostles, the prophets, the evangelists, the pastors and teachers, to equip his people for works of service, so that the body of Christ may be built up until we all reach unity in the faith and in the knowledge of the Son of God and become mature, attaining to the whole measure of the fullness of Christ.*

*Ephesians 4:11-13*

*From him the whole body, joined and held together by every supporting ligament, grows and builds itself up in love, as each part does its work.*

*Ephesians 4:16*

*Instead, speaking the truth in love, we will grow to become, in every respect the mature body of Him who is the head, that is Christ.*

*Ephesians 4:15*

*A new command I give you: Love one another. As I have loved you, so you must love one another. By this everyone will know that you are my disciples, if you love one another.*

*John 13:34-35*

*No one has ever seen God; but if we love one another, God lives in us and his love is made complete in us.*

*1 John 4:12*

*Husbands, you must love your wives so deeply, purely, and sacrificially that we can understand it only when we compare it to the love the Anointed One has for His bride, the church. We know He gave Himself up completely to make her His own, washing her clean of all her impurity with water and the powerful presence of His word. He has given Himself so that He can present the Church as His radiant bride, unstained, unwrinkled, and unblemished—completely free from all impurity—holy and innocent before Him.*

*Ephesians 5: 25-27 (The Voice)*

*The trumpeters and musicians <u>joined in unison to give praise and thanks</u> to the LORD. Accompanied by trumpets, cymbals and other instruments, the singers raised their voices in praise to the LORD and sang: "He is good; his love endures forever." Then the <u>temple of the LORD was filled with the cloud</u>, and the priests could not perform their service because of the cloud, for the glory of the LORD filled the temple of God.*

*2 Chronicles 5:13,14*

# FORMAT

This workbook is intended to help guide you in identifying any areas where you may need healing from situations that have damaged and interfered with your attitude or involvement with brothers or sisters in Christ or the Church. You can go through it on your own, or you can go through it with a trusted friend or facilitator. The workbook will walk you through prayers and questions to consider with the guidance of the Holy Spirit. Note that exercises 4 and 5 might not be necessary for you to go through, depending on your circumstances or background.

If you go through the workbook on your own, you can go at your own pace. Certain participants may find some of the questions to be redundant. This could especially be the case if there was an incident that was recent or tended to be more discouraging, in which case every question may seem to point back to that same event. Nevertheless, please persist in going through each question in its entirety and recognize that these questions are designed for instances where the mention of one specific word might trigger an emotion or memory.

In going through the questions, you might find that you easily get through several questions in a matter of minutes, and then have one question where it seems to take forever to go through or you get "stuck" and can't seem to move on from. Take the time to go through it thoroughly with Holy Spirit. He is the one who knows what you need to do and can bring about the revelation that leads to freedom. It's about getting healed, not finishing the book in one sitting. If you do find there are any questions you continue to struggle to get through or move on from, consider getting a friend or facilitator to help you, or if you discover there are feelings or thought patterns that are recurrent,

xxi

use those as an indicator that it might be a good time to participate in an individual inner healing session. In the preface, I mentioned participating in a *Sozo* session where a trained facilitator guides you through the process. Neil T. Anderson's *Freedom in Christ* and Rob Reimer's *Soul Care* are both worth mentioning for inner healing and can be used on your own or with a facilitator. If you do go through this Church Wounds workbook with a friend or facilitator, I would recommend the friend or facilitator be from another church body, if possible. This will decrease the chances of that person being familiar with the situations and people involved.

The format of the exercises will be relatively the same as you go through each exercise and question. After praying and inviting Holy Spirit to guide you and reveal anything that needs to be dealt with, you will read the question and answer it with whatever Holy Spirit shows you. Next, you will identify any lie(s) that you might have adopted because of this, and then pray a prayer of repentance, which basically means you confess that you have believed these lies and agree to replace them with truth and disallow them from negatively influencing you any further. The lies could be things we have perceived as truth but, in actuality are the way we have interpreted something, as demonstrated in the example I gave in the preface about my friend reading into my, "Good to see you here," comment. Rest assured I am not suggesting every issue is a result of you having misread something, but please also recognize this is something that should be considered. In cases where you have been mistreated, lies such as, "I'm not good enough", "Nobody appreciates me", or, "I can't deal with this," are what the enemy will use as a foothold.

Forgiving whoever played a part in mistreating you or contributing to you believing any lies will be the most important step in the process. "For if you forgive other people when they sin against you, your heavenly Father will also forgive you. But if you do not forgive others their sins, your Father will not forgive your sins." (Matthew 6:14,15). Jesus didn't lackadaisically suggest this practice, but He modeled it to the extreme that even after being betrayed, accused, arrested, denied, mocked, spit at, stripped, tortured beyond recognition, pierced by rusty nails, and hung on a cross to die, with heartfelt sincerity, He prayed, "Father, forgive them, for they do not know what they are doing" (Luke 23:34). We are called to follow Him, even when it's challenging. He takes the condition of our hearts seriously, and forgiveness is the only thing that brings cleansing to our souls. I suggest the forgiveness step look something like this: "I choose to forgive _____ (fill in the person's name) for _____ (state the offense(s) and making me feel _____ (identify the feelings associated with the offense). I release _____ (person's name) to You and ask You bless him/her."

Lastly you will ask God to present truth that relates to the situation, so that the lies you have believed can be replaced by His truths. We can trust what we hear is from God when it lines up with what He says in His Word.

---

Here's an example from Exercise 1, Question 1:

**1a) What misconceptions were you given in your growing up and developmental years about God? Jesus? Holy Spirit?**

*I was told that God was a disciplinarian and would punish me whenever I did something wrong.*

**1b) What lies might you have believed as a result? How may those lies have held you back in your spiritual walk? Repent of any lies you may have believed because of that.**

*I believed God was scary and mean. God, forgive me for believing the lie that you are mean and only want to intimidate and punish me. I acknowledge this is not right and I turn from this lie.*

**1c) Is there anybody you need to forgive for what happened? Pray a prayer of forgiveness for those that come to mind and those who contributed to you believing any lies.**

*I choose to forgive my grandpa for telling me this every time I did something wrong and making me fearful of God. I choose to forgive my grandma for emphasizing in teaching me about God, that He is a judge and punisher. I release them to You and ask You to bless them Lord.*

**1d) What truths does God want you to know?**

*That He is a God of grace and love. That He only ever disciplines out of perfect love. That my grandparents only knew how to follow God out of fear but perfect love drives out fear.*

Exercises 2-6 will include a question that asks how a situation made you feel. This question is intentional for a couple reasons. First, repressing and denying emotions has negative consequences. Like a barrel of toxic waste buried beneath the ground, over time the harmful content can leak out and contaminate everything around it. The expression 'feel it to heal it' allows us the opportunity to be honest with God and ourselves and bring our emotion to the light before the Lord. David was an excellent model of somebody who had a regular practice of doing this and he was called a man after God's own heart. If we are to experience Holy Spirit as a comforter, we must let Him have access to what needs comfort. Second, identifying how you feel can uncover patterns where inner healing is needed. For example, the first time I did an inner healing session, it became evident that my response to many situations was, "It made me feel rejected and like I wasn't good enough." This was beneficial to help me identify that I needed to deal with rejection issues and lack of worth that had arisen somewhere in my past. It also made me realize that when situations at church arose that made me feel that way, it wasn't necessarily that I was being wronged, but that this pre-existing sensitivity was getting activated.

---

Here's an example from Exercise 2, Question 1:

**1a) Do you feel you have been manipulated, mistreated, or abused within the church or one of its ministries? How?**
*I felt mistreated when I volunteered for years for free and was suddenly replaced by a full- time staff member.*

**1b) How did that make you feel?**
*I felt wronged and rejected because they didn't even consult me about replacing me, getting a job description, or what kind of person should be hired. I felt like all my free work was taken for granted and I felt like they were wasting money paying somebody to do the work full-time.*

**1c) What lies might you be believing as a result? How may those lies have held you back in your spiritual walk? Repent of any lies you may have believed because of that.**
*That I didn't do the job well enough and that the church is wasting money. I have been held back in that now I'm nervous to serve and don't want to give money to this church anymore. Lord, I repent of the lies that I didn't do well enough and that the church is necessarily wasting money.*

> **1d) Is there anybody you need to forgive for what happened? Pray a prayer of forgiveness for those that come to mind and those who contributed to you believing any lies.**
>
> *Lord, I choose to forgive the elders, especially Sam who I consider a friend, for replacing me and making me feel betrayed, rejected, taken for granted, and like I can't trust them. I release them to You and ask that You bless them Lord.*
>
> **1e) What truths does God want you to know?**
>
> *That I have been faithful, that I have gifts of service that are needed in the church, that I need to give up control of how I think things should be done because it's His church.*

Finally, at the end of each exercise two last questions will be given. The first is to encourage you to prayerfully consider whether it is necessary for you to go to a brother or sister who may have sinned against you, as Scripture recommends (Luke 17:3-4). This makes it clear there are certain times that approaching the offender is necessary, especially if that relationship requires a higher level of trust that needs to be restored in order for the relationship to be resumed at the same level. Let me be clear, I am not suggesting this should be done for each person you need to forgive, neither is it is my desire to teach or advise about when you should go to the person and when you should not. What I do suggest is asking Holy Spirit and if He prompts you, go prayerfully to the person and speak the truth in love (Ephesians 4:15), remembering what love is:

> "Love is patient, love is kind. It does not envy, it does not boast, it is not proud. It does not dishonor others, it is not self-seeking, it is not easily angered, it keeps no record of wrongs. Love does not delight in evil but rejoices with the truth. It always protects, always trusts, always hopes, always perseveres" (1 Corinthians 13:4-7).

The second of the last questions included toward the end of each of the exercises is there to determine if there is anybody you may have been the offender to (that is, you are the person somebody might have to forgive if they went through these questions). Ask Holy Spirit if you need to go to anybody to apologize to or reconcile with. "Therefore, if you are offering your gift at the altar and there remember that your brother or sister has something against you, leave your gift there in front of the altar. First go and be reconciled to them; then come and offer your gift" (Matthew 5:23,24).

*Instead, speaking the truth in love, we will grow to become in every respect the mature body of him who is the head, that is, Christ.*

*Ephesians 4:15*

*If your brother or sister sins against you, rebuke them; and if they repent, forgive them. Even if they sin against you seven times in a day and seven times come back to you saying, 'I repent,' you must forgive them."*

*Luke 17:3-4*

*"If your brother or sister sins, go and point out their fault, just between the two of you. If they listen to you, you have won them over. But if they will not listen, take one or two others along, so that 'every matter may be established by the testimony of two or three witnesses.' If they still refuse to listen, tell it to the church; and if they refuse to listen even to the church, treat them as you would a pagan or a tax collector.*

*Matthew 18:15-17*

CHAPTER

# 1

# THE FORMATIVE YEARS

WHAT HAPPENS TO US IN our developmental years is foundational in creating our understandings and perceptions of relationships and the world around us. It has been documented that even babies within the womb start attaining sensitivities about the world and their surroundings before they are born and cognitive of perceptions and situations.

For this reason, it can be beneficial to ask God if we might have any negative connotations with regards to God, Jesus, Holy Spirit, Christians, the Bible, or the Church, based on any childhood influences or experiences we had regardless of whether we were raised in a Christian home or not. These influences have the potential to create subconscious theological damage, apathy, skepticism, confusion, and/or resentment that can hold us back when it comes to living a Christian life.

Consider the child who was told by her father that the church is only after people's money. When she grows up, she may wonder why she experiences inner strife when she thinks about tithing or giving. What about the boy who was forced to memorize Scripture but wasn't successful at it and got shamed by the teacher? When he grows up and becomes a believer, he might not even recognize the correlation between that and his aversion to reading the Bible. Then there are the obvious detrimental circumstances that occur when a child or young person is abused within the church. Much healing is required for such an individual, and even those that have been associated with these victims or heard about such atrocities might also need to deal with the residual effects.

(***If you have been the victim of abuse within the church, whether physical or sexual, it is recommended that you go through an individual inner healing session with a trusted facilitator if you haven't done so already.)

# EXERCISE 1

## THE FORMATIVE YEARS

Begin by praying the following prayer:

*God, I recognize the value You have for Your Church, Your bride. Jesus, I acknowledge and thank you for the sacrifice You made for life, fullness, and freedom. Holy Spirit, I invite You to come and search me (you should pause here if you need to wait to sense His presence). Would You reveal and show me anything from my past that might be hindering me in any way from closeness with You and/or involvement with my brothers and sisters in Christ? Thank you that You want to bring these things to light and bring comfort and healing to my soul. In Jesus' Name. Amen*

1a) What misconceptions were you given in your growing up and developmental years about God? Jesus? Holy Spirit?

_____

_____

1b) What lies might you have believed as a result? (Reminder: The lies could be things you perceived as truth that could have arisen in the way you interpreted something or the lies could be from the thoughts that the situation instigated that the enemy wants you to replay in your mind). How may those lies have held you back in your spiritual walk? Repent of any lies you may have believed because of that.

_____

_____

1c) Is there anybody you need to forgive for what happened? Pray a prayer of forgiveness for those that come to mind and those who contributed to you believing any lies (Reminder, I suggest a prayer something like this: "I choose to forgive _____ (fill in the person's name) for _____ (state the offense(s) and making me feel _____ (identify the feelings associated with the offense). I release _____ (person's name) to You and ask You bless him/her. In Jesus' Name.")

_____

_____

1d) What truths does God want you to know?

_____

_____

2a) What are your earliest memories of the Bible? Do you have any bad memories related to the Bible?

_____

_____

2b) Are there any lies you might be believing correlated with these memories? Say a prayer of repentance for believing any lies.

_____

_____

2c) Is there anybody you need to forgive for what happened? Pray a prayer of forgiveness for those that come to mind and those who contributed to you believing any lies.

_____

_____

2d) What truths does God want you to know?

_____

_____

3a) What are your earliest memories about church? Are there any misconceptions you acquired with regards to what the church was like?

_____

_____

3b) What lies might you have believed because of these? Say a prayer of repentance for any lies you have believed.

_____

_____

3c) Is there anybody you need to forgive for what happened? Pray a prayer of forgiveness for those that come to mind and those who contributed to you believing any lies.

_____

_____

3d) What truths does God want you to know?

_____

_____

4a) Did you or anybody close to you have any bad experiences with church when you were growing up and in your developmental years? (Don't worry about justifying any bad experiences: if you perceived something to be a bad experience, there could easily be something you should deal with). What happened?

_____

_____

4b) Are there any lies you have believed because of that? Say a prayer of repentance for believing any lies.

_____

_____

4c) Is there anybody you need to forgive for what happened? Pray a prayer of forgiveness for those that come to mind and those who contributed to you believing any lies.

_____

_____

4d) What truths does God want you to know?

_____

_____

5a) As a child or young person, did you or anybody close to you have bad experiences with any Christians? What happened?

_____

_____

5b) Are there any lies you might have believed because of these? Say a prayer of repentance for believing any lies.

_____

_____

5c) Is there anybody you need to forgive for what happened? Pray a prayer of forgiveness for those that come to mind and those who contributed to you believing any lies.

_____

_____

5d) What truths does God want you to know?

_____

_____

***6) Lord, is there anybody that I need to go to privately and with love (as You describe in Scripture) to point out any of these offenses that came up, in order for reconciliation to occur?

_____

_____

***7) Lord, is there anybody I need to go to, to apologize for any offenses I may have incurred in any of these ways, in order for reconciliation to occur?

_____

_____

CHAPTER

# 2

# CHURCH EXPERIENCES

THOUGH SOME OF OUR WOUNDEDNESS may have come in our formative years, there are situations we encounter as teens or adults that stifle our zeal and leave spiritual scars. It's important to consider these circumstances and identify how they have impacted us or held us back in any way.

For example, I watched the passion and faith of a new believer dwindle when she was told she couldn't serve on a leadership team because she was living with her boyfriend. Now for as much as I support having leaders who are mature in their faith walk and setting a godly example to others, I also recognize that because of how this young lady was approached and treated, she sat in church feeling judged, shamed, and rejected instead of feeling cared for, protected, and accepted.

I have also seen well-meaning Christians practicing their faith and prayer tactics at the expense of another, like when a man in a wheelchair was approached and offered prayer and then told to stand in faith. I literally saw sweat on this man's forehead as he used every muscle in his upper body to try to hold up the weight of his listless bottom half in an attempt to stand; and then he was told he just needed more faith.

Then there's the practice of deliverance. Some have come to church leaders because they don't know where else to go. Some of these tortured individuals are ignored, made to feel crazy, or dismissed as unrealistic for considering the church could possibly offer any assistance but are recommended to seek the help of psychiatrists and doctors who simply hospitalize and medicate, while others are offered a deliverance session that may end up having them feeling practically physically tortured, yelled at, or shamed in some way. I have heard genuine deliverance providers humorously yet cautiously advise, "We don't want somebody needing deliverance because of our deliverance session."

The stories are endless; those who have experienced hypocrisy within the church, those who have been replaced by someone younger or with better abilities, those who have been taken advantage of, those who got betrayed, those who felt judged, misunderstood, criticized, accused, discouraged, neglected, offended, ignored, unsupported, unloved, mistreated, as well as those who have felt overlooked whether it was because of race, education, marital status, age, gender, or something else.

I have also heard endless stories of pastors and leaders who have been maligned and attacked because of decisions they have prayerfully made and usually sought wise counsel for.

Another factor in experiencing freedom due to church experiences relates to religiosity. Just as in Jesus' day there were the religious Pharisees, the blind guides, who implemented their manmade rules on the lay people, there are still preachers and laypeople today whose doctrine place laws and self-righteousness over love, soft-heartedness, and sensitivity to the Holy Spirit.

These can all leave a bad taste in our mouth when it comes to involvement in the body of Christ. We need spiritual mouthwash. Let's deal with it!

# EXERCISE 2

# PERSONAL CHURCH EXPERIENCE

Begin by praying the following prayer:

*God, I recognize the value You have for Your Church, Your bride. Forgive me for where I have dishonoured her. Thank you that Your forgiveness of my shortcomings is complete, and it allows me to experience freedom. Jesus, I acknowledge and thank you for the sacrifice You made for forgiveness, life, fullness, and freedom. Even when it is difficult, I know I can do all things (including forgiving others and honouring Your bride) because You strengthen me. Thank you, Holy Spirit, that in Your goodness You want to bring to light my woundedness so by Your strength I can forgive as You have forgiven me and You will bring comfort and healing to my soul. Holy Spirit, I invite You to come and search me (You should pause here if you need to wait to sense His presence). Come reveal and show me any experience I might have had that could be hindering me in any way from closeness with You and/or involvement with my brothers and sisters in Christ. In Jesus' Name. Amen*

1a) Do you feel you have been manipulated, mistreated, or abused within the church or one of its ministries? How?

_____

_____

1b) How did that make you feel?

_____

_____

1c) What lies might you have believed as a result? (Reminder: The lies could be things you perceived as truth that could have arisen in the way you interpreted something or the lies could be from the thoughts that the situation instigated that the enemy wants you to replay in your mind). How may those lies have held you back in your spiritual walk? Repent of any lies you may have believed because of that.

_____

_____

1d) Is there anybody you need to forgive for what happened? Pray a prayer of forgiveness for those that come to mind and those who contributed to you believing any lies (Reminder, I suggest a prayer something like this: "I choose to forgive _____ (fill in the person's name) for _____ (state the offense(s) and making me feel _____ (identify the feelings associated with the offense). I release _____ (person's name) to You and ask You bless him/her. In Jesus' Name.")

_____

_____

1e) What truths does God want you to know?

_____

_____

2a) How have you felt taken for granted or unappreciated within the church?

_____

_____

2b) How did that make you feel?

_____

_____

2c) What lies might that have resulted in you believing? How may those lies have held you back in your spiritual walk? Repent of any lies you may have believed because of that.

_____

_____

2d) Is there anybody you need to forgive for what happened? Pray a prayer of forgiveness for those that come to mind and those who contributed to you believing any lies.

_____

_____

2e) What truths does God want you to know?

_____

_____

3a) When have you felt criticized, offended, improperly disciplined, or judged by somebody within the church?

_____

_____

3b) How did that make you feel?

_____

_____

3c) What lies might that have resulted in you believing? How may those lies have held you back in your spiritual walk? Repent of any lies you may have believed because of that.

_____

_____

3d) Is there anybody you need to forgive for what happened? Pray a prayer of forgiveness for those that come to mind and those who contributed to you believing any lies.

_____

_____

3e) What truths does God want you to know?

_____

_____

4a) Do you feel like you have been lied to by somebody in the church?

_____

_____

4b) How did that make you feel?

_____

_____

4c) What lies might that have resulted in you believing? How may those lies have held you back in your spiritual walk? Repent of any lies you may have believed because of that.

_____

_____

4d) Is there anybody you need to forgive for what happened? Pray a prayer of forgiveness for those that come to mind and those who contributed to you believing any lies.

_____

_____

4e) What truths does God want you to know?

_____

_____

5a) How has the church or somebody within the church brought guilt or shame on you?

_____

_____

5b) How did that make you feel?

_____

_____

5c) What lies might that have resulted in you believing? How may those lies have held you back in your spiritual walk? Repent of any lies you may have believed because of that.

_____

_____

5d) Is there anybody you need to forgive for what happened? Pray a prayer of forgiveness for those that come to mind and those who contributed to you believing any lies.

_____

_____

5e) What truths does God want you to know?

_____

_____

6a) Do you feel a spiritual gift of yours has been overlooked or suppressed by somebody in the church?

6b) How did that make you feel?

6c) What lies might that have resulted in you believing? How may those lies have held you back in your spiritual walk? Repent of any lies you may have believed because of that.

6d) Is there anybody you need to forgive for what happened? Pray a prayer of forgiveness for those that come to mind and those who contributed to you believing any lies.

6e) What truths does God want you to know?

7a) Have you felt unaccepted or a sense of unbelonging within the body of Christ?

_____

_____

7b) How did that make you feel?

_____

_____

7c) What lies might that have resulted in you believing? How may those lies have held you back in your spiritual walk? Repent of any lies you may have believed because of that.

_____

_____

7d) Is there anybody you need to forgive for what happened? Pray a prayer of forgiveness for those that come to mind and those who contributed to you believing any lies.

_____

_____

7e) What truths does God want you to know?

_____

_____

8a) How do you feel the church has failed you?

_____

_____

8b) How did that make you feel?

_____

_____

8c) What lies might that have resulted in you believing? How may those lies have held you back in your spiritual walk? Repent of any lies you may have believed because of that.

_____

_____

8d) Is there anybody you need to forgive for what happened? Pray a prayer of forgiveness for those that come to mind and those who contributed to you believing any lies.

_____

_____

8e) What truths does God want you to know?

_____

_____

9a) Do you feel like the leadership in the church hasn't led you or fed you well or has wronged you or disappointed you?

 

9b) How did that make you feel?

 

9c) What lies might that have resulted in you believing? How may those lies have held you back in your spiritual walk? Repent of any lies you may have believed because of that.

 

9d) Is there anybody you need to forgive for what happened? Pray a prayer of forgiveness for those that come to mind and those who contributed to you believing any lies.

 

9e) What truths does God want you to know?

10a) Do you harbor frustration regarding a ministry or program, in how it's run, or how it's not run, or how you were treated?

_____

_____

10b) How did that make you feel?

_____

_____

10c) What lies might that have resulted in you believing? How may those lies have held you back in your spiritual walk? Repent of any lies you may have believed because of that.

_____

_____

10d) Is there anybody you need to forgive for what happened? Pray a prayer of forgiveness for those that come to mind and those who contributed to you believing any lies.

_____

_____

10e) What truths does God want you to know?

_____

_____

11a) What religious instructions or mandates have you been taught that might be deemed as manmade rules as opposed to God's instructions?

11b) How did that make you feel?

11c) What lies might that have resulted in you believing? How may those lies have held you back in your spiritual walk? Repent of any lies you may have believed becauses of that.

11d) Is there anybody you need to forgive for what happened? Pray a prayer of forgiveness for those that come to mind and those who contributed to you believing any lies.

11e) What truths does God want you to know?

12a) How have you experienced hypocrisy within the church?

_____

_____

12b) How did that make you feel?

_____

_____

12c) What lies might that have resulted in you believing? How may those lies have held you back in your spiritual walk? Repent of any lies you may have believed because of that.

_____

_____

12d) Is there anybody you need to forgive for what happened? Pray a prayer of forgiveness for those that come to mind and those who contributed to you believing any lies.

_____

_____

12e) What truth does God want you to know?

_____

_____

13a) Has anybody given you a prophetic word that seemed inaccurate, inappropriate, or caused you fear or angst?

_____

_____

13b) How did that make you feel?

_____

_____

13c) What lies might that have resulted in you believing? How may those lies have held you back in your spiritual walk? Repent of any lies you may have believed because of that.

_____

_____

13d) Is there anybody you need to forgive for what happened? Pray a prayer of forgiveness for those that come to mind and those who contributed to you believing any lies.

_____

_____

13e) What truths does God want you to know?

_____

_____

14a) Do you feel that any of your brothers or sisters in Christ have tempted you or been a stumbling block to you in your walk with the Lord (examples: through unwholesome talk, critical attitudes, judgment, over-indulgences, finances, vanity, materialism, sexual temptations, justifying sin etc.)?

---

---

14b) How did that make you feel?

---

---

14c) What lies might that have resulted in you believing? How may those lies have held you back in your spiritual walk? Repent of any lies you may have believed because of that.

---

---

14d) Is there anybody you need to forgive for what happened? Pray a prayer of forgiveness for those that come to mind and those who contributed to you believing any lies.

---

---

14e) What truths does God want you to know?

---

---

15a) Is there anybody in the church you have been jealous of, critical of, judgmental of, may have mistreated, been cold towards, or offended?

_____

_____

15b) How does that make you feel?

_____

_____

15c) What lies might you be believing associated with any of these? How may those lies have held you back in your spiritual walk? Repent of any lies you may have believed because of that.

_____

_____

15d) Is there anybody you need to forgive for what happened? Pray a prayer of forgiveness for those that come to mind and those who contributed to you believing any lies.

_____

_____

15e) What truths does God want you to know?

_____

_____

***16) Lord, is there anybody that I need to go to privately and with love (as You describe in Scripture) to point out any of these offenses that came up, in order to make reconciliation?

_____

_____

***17) Lord, is there anybody I need to go to, to apologize for any offenses I may have incurred in any of these ways, in order to make reconciliation?

_____

_____

CHAPTER

# 3

# WITNESSING THE CHURCH EXPERIENCES OF OTHERS

WE JUST WENT THROUGH PERSONAL experiences you may have encountered that might have contributed to any woundedness with the church. The next section will involve identifying if anything you have perceived that the church or Christians may have done to others has caused any level of hurt or frustration to you. Again, the enemy wants to get a foothold by any means possible, and for people who have a level of altruism or protectiveness in them, they can be hurt more by what happens to others than what happens to themselves. Like the parent who acknowledges, "You might be able to mess with me but if you mess with my children, you will experience zero-to-psycho in a blink of an eye," second-hand offenses are a real issue.

There was a couple I knew where the wife was a believer, and the husband was not. In their well-meaningness, some people from her church took it upon themselves to approach the husband and suggest he could be more supportive of his wife if he just came to church with her from time to time. He told them he wasn't interested, and genuinely he wasn't offended by the actions of these spiritual "busy bodies". However, when the wife found out what they had done, she was upset they would do that to him, and harbored resentment and mistrust because of it.

What can we learn from Jesus about this subject? First, we are instructed with the well-known teaching from the Sermon on the Mount, "For if you forgive other people for their offenses, your heavenly Father will also forgive you. But if you do not forgive other people, then your Father will not forgive your offenses." (Matthew 6:14-15, NASB). Second, Luke 12:13 gives us an example: "Now someone in the crowd said to Him, "Teacher, tell my brother to divide the family inheritance with me." But He said to him, "You there—who appointed Me a judge or arbitrator over the two of you?" (NASB). If Jesus wasn't willing make Himself a judge in their situation, what right would we have? No wonder He taught later in the Sermon on the Mount recorded in Matthew 7:

> "Do not judge, or you too will be judged. For in the way you judge others, you will be judged, and with the measure you use, it will be measured to you. Why do you look at the speck of sawdust in your brother's eye and pay no attention to the plank in your own eye? How can you say to your brother, 'Let me take the speck out of your eye,' when all the time there's a plank in your own eye? You hypocrite, first take the plank out of your own eye, and then you will see clearly to take the speck from your brother's eye."

Not only are we not in any position to judge others, but we must always remember there are three sides to every story; his perspective, her perspective, and the actual truth, which tends to land somewhere in between.

EXERCISE 3

# WITNESSING THE CHURCH EXPERIENCES OF OTHERS

Begin by praying the following prayer:

*God, I recognize the value You have for Your Church, Your bride. Forgive me for where I have dishonoured her. Thank you that Your forgiveness of my shortcomings is complete, and it allows me to experience freedom. Jesus, I acknowledge and thank you for the sacrifice You made for forgiveness, life, fullness, and freedom. Even when it is difficult, I know I can do all things (including forgiving others and honouring Your bride) because You strengthen me. Thank you, Holy Spirit, that in Your goodness You want to bring to light my woundedness so by Your strength I can forgive as You have forgiven me and You will bring comfort and healing to my soul. Holy Spirit, I invite You to come and search me (You can pause here if you need to wait to sense His presence). Would You reveal and show me any experience somebody I know or care for might have had that could be hindering me in any way from closeness with You and/or closeness with my brothers and sisters in Christ? Thank you that You want to bring these things to light and bring comfort and healing to my soul. In Jesus' Name. Amen*

1a) Do you feel somebody you know or care for has been manipulated, mistreated, or abused within the church or one of its ministries?

_____

_____

1b) What lies might you have believed as a result? (Reminder: The lies could be things you perceived as truth that could have arisen in the way you interpreted something or the lies could be from the thoughts that the situation instigated that the enemy wants you to replay in your mind).

_____

_____

1c) How may those lies have held you back in your spiritual walk? Repent of any lies you may have believed because of that.

_____

_____

1d) Is there anybody you need to forgive for what happened? Pray a prayer of forgiveness for those that come to mind and those who contributed to you believing any lies (Reminder, I suggest a prayer something like this: "I choose to forgive _____ (fill in the person's name) for _____ (state the offense(s) and making me feel _____ (identify the feelings associated with the offense). I release _____ (person's name) to You and ask You bless him/her. In Jesus' Name.")

_____

_____

1e) What truths does God want you to know?

_____

_____

2a) How has somebody you know or care for been taken for granted or unappreciated within the church?

2b) What lies might that have resulted in you believing?

2c) How may those lies have held you back in your spiritual walk? Repent of any lies you may have believed because of that.

2d) Is there anybody you need to forgive for what happened? Pray a prayer of forgiveness for those that come to mind and those who contributed to you believing any lies.

2e) What truths does God want you to know?

3a) When has somebody you know or cared for felt criticized, offended, improperly disciplined, or judged by somebody else within the church?

_____

_____

3b) What lies might that have resulted in you believing?

_____

_____

3c) How may those lies have held you back in your spiritual walk? Repent of any lies you may have believed because of that.

_____

_____

3d) Is there anybody you need to forgive for what happened? Pray a prayer of forgiveness for those that come to mind and those who contributed to you believing any lies.

_____

_____

3e) What truths does God want you to know?

_____

_____

4a) Do you feel like somebody you know or care for has been lied to by somebody else in the church?

_____

_____

4b) What lies might that have resulted in you believing?

_____

_____

4c) How may those lies have held you back in your spiritual walk? Repent of any lies you may have believed because of that.

_____

_____

4d) Is there anybody you need to forgive for what happened? Pray a prayer of forgiveness for those that come to mind and those who contributed to you believing any lies.

_____

_____

4e) What truths does God want you to know?

_____

_____

5a) How has the church or somebody within the church brought guilt or shame on somebody you know or care for?

_____

_____

5b) What lies might that have resulted in you believing?

_____

_____

5c) How may those lies have held you back in your spiritual walk? Repent of any lies you may have believed because of that.

_____

_____

5d) Is there anybody you need to forgive for what happened? Pray a prayer of forgiveness for those that come to mind and those who contributed to you believing any lies.

_____

_____

5e) What truths does God want you to know?

_____

_____

6a) Do you feel a gift of somebody you know or care for has been overlooked or squelched by somebody in the church?

6b) What lies might that have resulted in you believing?

6c) How may those lies have held you back in your spiritual walk? Repent of any lies you may have believed because of that.

6d) Is there anybody you need to forgive for what happened? Pray a prayer of forgiveness for those that come to mind and those who contributed to you believing any lies.

6e) What truths does God want you to know?

7a) Do you feel somebody you know or care for has felt unaccepted or a sense of unbelonging within the body of Christ?

_____

_____

7b) What lies might that have resulted in you believing?

_____

_____

7c) How may those lies have held you back in your spiritual walk? Repent of any lies you may have believed because of that.

_____

_____

7d) Is there anybody you need to forgive for what happened? Pray a prayer of forgiveness for those that come to mind and those who contributed to you believing any lies.

_____

_____

7e) What truths does God want you to know?

_____

_____

8a) How do you feel the church has failed somebody you know or care for?

_____

_____

8b) What lies might that have resulted in you believing?

_____

_____

8c) How may those lies have held you back in your spiritual walk? Repent of any lies you may have believed because of that.

_____

_____

8d) Is there anybody you need to forgive for what happened? Pray a prayer of forgiveness for those that come to mind and those who contributed to you believing any lies.

_____

_____

8e) What truths does God want you to know?

_____

_____

9a) Do you feel like the leadership in the church hasn't led somebody you know or care for well, or has mistreated them or been a disappointment to them?

_____

_____

9b) What lies might that have resulted in you believing?

_____

_____

9c) How may those lies have held you back in your spiritual walk? Repent of any lies you may have believed because of that.

_____

_____

9d) Is there anybody you need to forgive for what happened? Pray a prayer of forgiveness for those that come to mind and those who contributed to you believing any lies.

_____

_____

9e) What truths does God want you to know?

_____

_____

10a) Does somebody you know or care for harbor frustration regarding a ministry or program, in how it's run, or how it's not run, or how he/she was treated?

_____

_____

10b) What lies might that have resulted in you believing?

_____

_____

10c) How may those lies have held you back in your spiritual walk? Repent of any lies you may have believed because of that.

_____

_____

10d) Is there anybody you need to forgive for what happened? Pray a prayer of forgiveness for those that come to mind and those who contributed to you believing any lies.

_____

_____

10e) What truths does God want you to know?

_____

_____

CHURCH WOUNDS | 41

11a) What religious instructions or mandates has somebody you know or care for been taught that might fall into manmade rules as opposed to God's instructions?

_____

_____

11b) What lies might that have resulted in you believing?

_____

_____

11c) How may those lies have held you back in your spiritual walk? Repent of any lies you may have believed because of that.

_____

_____

11d) Is there anybody you need to forgive for what happened? Pray a prayer of forgiveness for those that come to mind and those who contributed to you believing any lies.

_____

_____

11e) What truths does God want you to know?

_____

_____

12a) How has somebody you know or care for experienced hypocrisy within the church?

_____

_____

12b) What lies might that have resulted in you believing?

_____

_____

12c) How may those lies have held you back in your spiritual walk? Repent of any lies you may have believed because of that.

_____

_____

12d) Is there anybody you need to forgive for what happened? Pray a prayer of forgiveness for those that come to mind and those who contributed to you believing any lies.

_____

_____

12e) What truths does God want you to know?

_____

_____

13a) Has anybody given a person you know or care for a prophetic word that seemed inaccurate, inappropriate, or caused you fear or angst?

_____

_____

13b) What lies might that have resulted in you believing?

_____

_____

13c) How may those lies have held you back in your spiritual walk? Repent of any lies you may have believed because of that.

_____

_____

13d) Is there anybody you need to forgive for what happened? Pray a prayer of forgiveness for those that come to mind and those who contributed to you believing any lies.

_____

_____

13e) What truths does God want you to know?

_____

_____

14a) Do you feel that any of your brothers or sisters in Christ have tempted somebody you know or care for, or been a stumbling block to him/her in their walk with the Lord (examples: through gossip, criticism, judgment, over-indulgences, vanity, materialism, sexual temptation, etc.)?

_____

_____

14b) What lies might that have resulted in you believing?

_____

_____

14c) How may those lies have held you back in your spiritual walk? Repent of any lies you may have believed because of that.

_____

_____

14d) Is there anybody you need to forgive for what happened? Pray a prayer of forgiveness for those that come to mind and those who contributed to you believing any lies.

_____

_____

14e) What truths does God want you to know?

_____

_____

15a) Is there anybody in the church somebody you know or care for has been jealous of, critical of, judgmental of, has mistreated, been cold towards, or offended?

_____

_____

15b) What lies might you be believing associated with any of these?

_____

_____

15c) How may those lies have held you back in your spiritual walk? Repent of any lies you may have believed because of that.

_____

_____

15d) Is there anybody you need to forgive for what happened? Pray a prayer of forgiveness for those that come to mind and those who contributed to you believing any lies.

_____

_____

15e) What truths does God want you to know?

_____

_____

***16) Lord, is there anybody that I need to go to privately and with love (as You describe in Scripture) to point out any of these offenses that came up, in order to make reconciliation?

---

---

***17) Lord, is there anybody I need to go to, to apologize for an offense I may have incurred in any of these ways, in order to make reconciliation?

---

---

# CHAPTER

# 4

# SERVING IN LEADERSHIP

I AM SO THANKFUL FOR those that walk in their gifts since, "Christ himself gave the apostles, the prophets, the evangelists, the pastors and teachers, to equip his people for works of service, so that the body of Christ may be built up." (Ephesians 4:11-12)

Those who serve in any capacity of leadership within a church organization have even more opportunities for woundedness to occur since they are in a bit of a spotlight and often somewhat of a magnifying glass. They are more likely to be scrutinized, criticized, talked about, held accountable, approached, confronted, disagreed with, complained to, complained about, and compared to others.

In Luke 17, there is a warning for those who may cause people to stumble. It could be argued that this could be an intentional warning for teachers and leaders since they have more opportunities through their position to influence others. James 3:1 confirms that teachers will indeed be judged more strictly. Returning to Luke 17 though, after the warning to be cautious not to cause little ones to stumble, there is further instruction about specifically forgiving others. It's as if Jesus was warning those with such influence that they in particular would have to forgive others, regularly and repeatedly.

---

*Jesus said to his disciples: "Things that cause people to stumble are bound to come, but woe to anyone through whom they come. It would be better for them to be thrown into the sea with a millstone tied around their neck than to cause one of these little ones to stumble. So watch yourselves.*

*"If your brother or sister sins against you, rebuke them; and if they repent, forgive them. Even if they sin against you seven times in a day and seven times come back to you saying, 'I repent,' you must forgive them."*

*Luke 17:1-4*

# EXERCISE 4

# SERVING IN LEADERSHIP

Begin by praying the following prayer:

*God, I recognize gifts You have given me to lead others so that Your body may be built up. Jesus, I acknowledge and thank you for Your perfect example in leadership. Holy Spirit, I praise You that you are with me and teach me and equip me for your service. Would you reveal and show me any experiences where I have been specifically wounded because of my place of leadership, so I can forgive as God has forgiven me through Christ? Thank you that You want to bring these things to light and bring comfort and healing to my soul. In Jesus' Name. Amen*

1a) Have you felt undermined, micromanaged, bullied, or controlled?

_____

_____

1b) How did that make you feel?

_____

_____

1c) What lies might you have believed as a result? (Reminder: The lies could be things you perceived as truth that could have arisen in the way you interpreted something or the lies could be from the thoughts that the situation instigated that the enemy wants you to replay in your mind). How may those lies have held you back in your spiritual walk? Repent of any lies you may have believed because of that.

_____

_____

1d) Is there anybody you need to forgive for what happened? Pray a prayer of forgiveness for those that come to mind and those who contributed to you believing any lies (Reminder, I suggest a prayer something like this: "I choose to forgive _____ (fill in the person's name) for _____ (state the offense(s) and making me feel _____ (identify the feelings associated with the offense). I release _____ (person's name) to You and ask You bless him/her. In Jesus' Name.")

_____

_____

1e) What truths does God want you to know?

_____

_____

2a) Have you ever been removed from or replaced in leadership?

_____

_____

2b) How did that make you feel?

_____

_____

2c) What lies might that have caused you to believe? Repent of any lies you may have believed because of that.

_____

_____

2d) Is there anybody you need to forgive for what happened? Pray a prayer of forgiveness for those that come to mind and those who contributed to you believing lies.

_____

_____

2e) What truths does God want you to know?

_____

_____

3a) Have you felt betrayed by those you have served or served with?

---

---

3b) How did that make you feel?

---

---

3c) What lies might that have caused you to believe? Repent of any lies you may have believed because of that.

---

---

3d) Is there anybody you need to forgive for what happened? Pray a prayer of forgiveness for those that come to mind and those who contributed to you believing lies.

---

---

3e) What truths does God want you to know?

---

---

4a) Have you ever felt burdened by unrealistic expectations and demands?

4b) How did that make you feel?

4c) What lies might that have caused you to believe? Repent of any lies you may have believed because of that.

4d) Is there anybody you need to forgive for what happened? Pray a prayer of forgiveness for those that come to mind and those who contributed to you believing any lies.

4e) What truths does God want you to know?

5a) Have you felt unsupported or alone in your ministry?

5b) How did that make you feel?

5c) What lies might that have caused you to believe? Repent of any lies you may have believed because of that.

5d) Is there anybody you need to forgive for what happened? Pray a prayer of forgiveness for those that come to mind and those who contributed to you believing any lies.

5e) What truths does God want you to know?

6a) Have accusations been made against you?

_____

_____

6b) How did that make you feel?

_____

_____

6c) What lies might that have caused you to believe? Repent of any lies you may have believed because of that.

_____

_____

6d) Is there anybody you need to forgive for what happened? Pray a prayer of forgiveness for those that come to mind and those who contributed to you believing any lies.

_____

_____

6e) What truths does God want you to know?

_____

_____

7a) Do you feel your leadership wasn't appreciated or valued?

 

7b) How did that make you feel?

 

7c) What lies might that have caused you to believe? Repent of any lies you may have believed because of that.

 

7d) Is there anybody you need to forgive for what happened? Pray a prayer of forgiveness for those that come to mind and those who contributed to you believing any lies.

 

7e) What truths does God want you to know?

8a) Is there a peer (that is, another person in the same kind of leadership you have) that you feel has discredited your ministry position, your church, or your denomination because of their words or actions?

8b) How did that make you feel?

8c) What lies might it have caused you to believe? Repent of any lies you may have believed because of that.

8d) Is there anybody you need to forgive for what happened? Pray a prayer of forgiveness for those that come to mind and those who contributed to you believing any lies.

8e) What truths does God want you to know?

***9) Lord, is there anybody that I need to go to privately and with love (as You describe in Scripture) to point out any of these offenses that came up, in order to make reconciliation?

_____

_____

***10) Lord, is there anybody I need to go to, to apologize for an offense I may have incurred in any of these ways, in order to make reconciliation?

_____

_____

CHAPTER

# 5

## FAMILY RELATIONSHIPS WITH CHURCH LEADERS (PAID OR VOLUNTEER)

THOSE WHO ARE MARRIED TO or are children of church leaders can have different kinds of woundedness. Spouses or family members often feel the heartache of seeing their loved one mistreated by people in the church, the same people who are called to, "love others as themselves" (Mark 12:31), and to, "respect those who labor among you and are over you in the Lord and admonish you, and to esteem them very highly in love because of their work" (1 Thessalonians 5:12-13). This has the potential to lead to feelings of anger, defenselessness, anxiety, rebellion, mistrust, and/or abandoning the Church or God altogether. If this has been the case for you, hopefully you were able to address some of these things in Exercise 3.

The situations we haven't addressed yet come in the form of "pastor's kids" or the spouses of leaders who have felt the burdens of ministry. There may have been expectations to live up to a certain standard because of who their parent or spouse was. There may have been demands on time and finances. There were likely many sacrifices.

Yet again, there is a different kind of hurt that may have come to family members or spouses who have lived with and witnessed first-hand neglect, abuse, or hypocrisy exhibited by what others might deem a godly and respected leader.

## EXERCISE 5

# FAMILY RELATIONSHIPS
# WITH CHURCH LEADERS
# (PAID OR VOLUNTEER)

Begin by praying the following prayer:

*God, you have called imperfect people to be your hands and feet in this world. Jesus, you were the perfect example by practicing what you preached, but I admit that in living with a Church leader, I have experienced firsthand some of the imperfections and inconsistencies in the behaviour of those who call themselves Christians. Holy Spirit, I praise you that You are genuine, and You want my heart and attitude to be genuine. Would You reveal and show me any experiences where I have been specifically wounded because of my close relationship with my spouse or parent who is (or was) a Church leader, so I can forgive as God has forgiven me through Christ? Thank you that You want to bring these things to light so I can walk in Your freedom. In Jesus' Name. Amen*

1a) Have you felt neglected by your spouse/parent? Or like the people in the church took priority over you?

_____

_____

1b) How did that make you feel?

_____

_____

1c) What lies might you have believed as a result? (Reminder: The lies could be things you perceived as truth that could have arisen in the way you interpreted something or the lies could be from the thoughts that the situation instigated that the enemy wants you to replay in your mind). How may those lies have held you back in your spiritual walk? Repent of any lies you may have believed because of that.

_____

_____

1d) Is there anybody you need to forgive for what happened? Pray a prayer of forgiveness for those that come to mind and those who contributed to you believing any lies (Reminder, I suggest a prayer something like this: "I choose to forgive _____ (fill in the person's name) for _____ (state the offense(s) and making me feel _____ (identify the feelings associated with the offense). I release _____ (person's name) to You and ask You bless him/her. In Jesus' Name.")

_____

_____

1e) What truths does God want you to know?

_____

_____

2a) Do you feel like you had to make unfair sacrifices because of your family member's position? What were they?

_____

_____

2b) How did that make you feel?

_____

_____

2c) What lies might that have caused you to believe? Repent of any lies you may have believed because of that.

_____

_____

2d) Who do you need to forgive for this? Forgive any people associated with you believing those lies.

_____

_____

2e) What truths does God want you to know?

_____

_____

3a) Did you feel pressure, embarrassment, or resentment because of your family member's position? What did that look like?

_____

_____

3b) How did that make you feel?

_____

_____

3c) What lies might that have caused you to believe? Repent of any lies you may have believed because of that.

_____

_____

3d) Who do you need to forgive for this? Forgive any people associated with you believing those lies.

_____

_____

3e) What truths does God want you to know?

_____

_____

4a) Have you ever felt like your family member has been hypocritical? In what way?

_____

_____

4b) How did that make you feel?

_____

_____

4c) What lies might that have caused you to believe? Repent of any lies you may have believed because of that.

_____

_____

4d) Who do you need to forgive for this? Forgive any people associated with you believing those lies.

_____

_____

4e) What truths does God want you to know?

_____

_____

5a) Do you feel like your family member has given you a bad taste of what church or a Christian is supposed to look like?

_____

_____

5b) How did that make you feel?

_____

_____

5c) What lies might that have caused you to believe? Repent of any lies you may have believed because of that.

_____

_____

5d) Who do you need to forgive for this? Forgive any people associated with you believing those lies.

_____

_____

5e) What truths does God want you to know?

_____

_____

6a) Have you seen your spouse/parent mistreated by others in the church? Do you feel like you dealt with this in Exercise 3 already? If not, please continue.

_____

_____

6b) What happened? How did that make you feel?

_____

_____

6c) What lies might that have caused you to believe? Repent of any lies you may have believed because of that.

_____

_____

6d) Who do you need to forgive for this? Forgive any people associated with you believing those lies.

_____

_____

6e) What truths does God want you to know?

_____

_____

\*\*\*7) Lord, is there anybody that I need to go to privately and with love (as You describe in Scripture) to point out any of these offenses that came up, in order for reconciliation to occur?

---

---

CHAPTER

# 6

## BLAMING GOD

BECAUSE WE LIVE IN A broken world, there is sickness, addiction, poverty, famine, slavery, controversy, war, natural disaster, and death. This was not God's plan for the world, but it is by His goodness and grace that we can have hope, joy, and fullness, in spite of the condition of the world. In knowing that God is the Creator and that He is all-powerful, many people have placed blame on God for hardships, especially when one of those hardships becomes personal and closer to home. This is where we need to identify if we need to repent of any resentment or lies we are believing about God. We need to come back to the truth about God's nature and character. We must be vigilant in remembering that good vs evil is not just a theme from a movie but there is a real enemy who is out to steal, kill, and destroy us (John 10:10), and since the garden of Eden has been on a mission to convince mankind to doubt God, persuade us that God might be holding out on us, and get us to rebel against God by living our lives independently of Him, morally or immorally. God powerfully created free-will, but we must be aware and accept that free-will comes with consequences here on earth, and eternally.

Obviously, if we are holding a grudge against God, it will affect our faith, relationships, and desire for connection within the Church.

Thankfully, God demonstrated His good, caring, loving, and generous nature by sending His one and only Son, Jesus, a person who lived perfectly and demonstrated to us what life, love, and relationships are supposed to look like, so whoever believes in Him can have everlasting life (John 3:16). God is that good, so devised a redemption plan for us. The sin, darkness, and rebellion that originated in the garden of Eden causing a chasm between mankind and God was reconciled through Jesus. Sinless, He died on the cross as a sacrifice for sin so separation from God would no longer prevail for those who confess their imperfections, believe in what He did for them, and accept Him and His ways. He exemplified forgiveness as, while enduring the gruesome torture of hanging on a cross, He prayed for those persecuting Him saying, "Father, forgive them, for they do not know what they are doing." (Luke 23:34). He modelled forgiveness to us and not once did He blame God for His pain or suffering.

God is perfect, holy, and full of love. He does no wrong (Deuteronomy 32:4). Good only exists because of Him. Because of this, it is unwarranted for us to blame Him for things that have gone wrong. Some people propose that we need to consider forgiving God for where we have blamed Him, which makes sense in that we are called to forgive others, but it also doesn't make sense in that He is perfect and therefore has done nothing wrong. Identify what you need to do for yourself and your own freedom. What is most important is that we figure out what lies we have been believing about Him and replace them with what is true, because we know it is the truth that sets us free (John 8:32).

# EXERCISE 6

# BLAMING GOD

Begin by praying the following prayer:

*God, I praise You because You are perfect in all that You are and all that You do. Your ways and understanding are higher than I could ever imagine. Your love, mercy, and goodness are abundant. I confess I am a sinner; please forgive me for where I have lived apart from You and believed lies about You. Jesus, thank you for your sacrifice on the cross for my sins. Thank you for being the example on earth of what it looks like to live righteously, forgivingly, and connected to God. I invite You into my life to purify me and make me like You. Holy Spirit, thank you that you have God's best intentions in mind for me and I invite you now to come fill me (you can pause here if you need to wait to sense His presence) and search my heart and reveal anything I might be blaming God for or if I am believing the lie that He is holding back from me in any way. Thank you that you want my connection with God close and unhindered. In Jesus' Name. Amen*

1a) Do you feel like God has let you down in any way?

_____

_____

1b) How does that make you feel?

_____

_____

1c) Since God is faithful, good, and never forsakes us, what lies have you been believing? (Reminder: The lies could be things we perceived as truth that could have arisen in the way we interpreted something or the lies could be from the thoughts that the situation instigated that the enemy wants us to replay in minds). Repent of any lies you may have believed.

_____

_____

1d) Is there anybody you need to forgive for influencing you to believe these lies? Forgive any people associated with you believing these lies. (Reminder, I recommend the forgiveness prayer look something like this: "I choose to forgive _____ (fill in the person's name) for _____ (state the offense(s) and making me feel _____ (identify the feelings associated with the offense). I release _____ (person's name) to You and ask You bless him/her. In Jesus' Name.")

_____

_____

1e) Do you feel like it would be helpful for you to pray to forgive God? If you do, do so now.

_____

_____

1f) What truths does God want you to know? Is there anything else He wants you to know?

_____

_____

# IN CONCLUSION

After going through the exercises in this workbook, my prayer is that you have received breakthrough in healing and that this freedom will bear fruit in love, joy, peace, patience, kindness, and grace, that will in turn promote unity within the Church.

There are two things worth mentioning as we conclude. First, as we finish going through the exercises in this workbook, it might become evident that some of the offenses came about because of the way we perceived something or because of our own sensitivities or insecurities. If you noticed there was any issue that seemed to repeat itself (for example, perhaps you noticed it has been continual that you have felt criticized or rejected in the church), I highly recommend an individual inner healing session to dig further into past wounds that are quite possibly just being revealed through church situations but have more to do with personal woundedness than church woundedness.

Second, completing these exercises doesn't mean you are necessarily done altogether (sorry). You may still need to go to somebody in love to discuss any issues you have with them, or that they might have with you. In addition, this might be the time for you to prayerfully consider if you need to do something different with regards to church or relationships with any Christians (eg. Change in attitude, start attending a church again, change churches, implement healthy boundaries etc.) Finally, you might need to review these exercises again in the near future either because there can be more layers to healing (the perfect scenario is that we could be completely healed and check it off our list as done, but inner healing has a way of going deeper as we grow in maturity) or because any recent predicaments need to be dealt with.

It is my prayer that we will walk freely and in wholeness so we can experience and demonstrate the radical love, unity, peace, joy, strength, power, and fullness, that God intends for us and that the world is hungry for.

*Jesus prayed: "Holy Father, protect them by the power of Your name, the name You gave me, so that they may be one as we are one. Sanctify them by the truth; your word is truth. As you sent me into the world, I have sent them into the world. For them I sanctify myself, that they too may be truly sanctified. My prayer is not for them alone. I pray also for those who will believe in me through their message, that all of them may be one, Father, just as you are in me and I am in you. May they also be in us so that the world may believe that you have sent me."*

*John 17:11(b), 17-21*

*How good and pleasant it is when God's people live together in unity!*

*Psalm 133:1*